FLEEING THE WAR IN UKRAINE!

SUDDENLY BECOMING A TEENAGE REFUGEE

WRITTEN BY
JULIA LOVE

ILLUSTRATED BY
ANGELICA RODRIGUEZ

Ark House Press
arkhousepress.com

Unless otherwise stated, all Scriptures are taken from the New International Translation (Holy Bible. Copyright© 1996, 2004, 2007, 2013 by Tyndale House Foundation. Used by permission of Tyndale House Publishers Inc., Carol Stream, Illinois 60188. All rights reserved.)

Some names and identifying details have been changed to protect the privacy of individuals.

Cataloguing in Publication Data:
Title: Fleeing The War In Ukraine! *Suddenly Becoming A Teenage Refugee*
ISBN: 978-0-6459938-0-6 (pbk)
Subjects: YOUNG ADULT FICTION / Action & Adventure / Survival Stories; YOUNG ADULT FICTION / People & Places / Europe; YOUNG ADULT FICTION / Religious / Christian / Social Issues;
Other Authors/Contributors: Love, Julia; Rodriguez, Angelica;

Design by initiateagency.com

CHAPTER 1

Sveta was jolted awake by an enormous bang and crash in her room. The bed shook and the walls of her small bedroom seemed to be still vibrating.

"What's happening?" "What's going on?" she screamed, as a baby's urgent crying, not so far away, pierced the chilly air.

Dawn was just breaking, so she could now see that some of the glass in her window was broken and the rest, lay in jagged pieces on the floor near her bed. Ginger, her cat had leapt off her bed in terror. He still looked rather scared and they both nervously looked around in the semi darkness of the room.

Suddenly, Dad, Mum and her little brother Sergy burst through the door to make sure she was alive and well, after the blast.

"Are you alright Sveta?" Mum asked with a worried look. Sergy asked innocently, "What did you do Sveta?" She nodded silently to her Mum's question but didn't bother answering Sergy.

Gazing out the half-broken window, Dad explained "A Russian bomb or missile must have hit the next-door block of flats, just across from your window. Look over there at all the damage!"

There was an enormous black hole in the side of that building and the cold, early morning air was now filled with further wailing and muffled screams.

Sergy began to sob loudly. Then all the family, in their shock and feelings of helplessness, had a long group hug. They all tried to comfort 5-year-old Sergy, who hadn't stopped crying, and Patch their terrier dog, who continued his urgent barking.

Sadly, they knew that this type of disaster was becoming more and more common in their once peaceful town, in the north eastern part of Ukraine. In the last few weeks, the sound of explosions and gunshots in the distance were becoming louder and louder, closer and closer.

At first, everybody had tried to ignore it and keep up their normal daily activities. At 13, Sveta had always enjoyed a happy life. Her parents both had good jobs and their flat was always warm and snug. She loved school and had some great friends, with whom she often enjoyed playing around in the snow each winter.

However, Sveta and Sergy already had some idea that their quiet, peaceful life was over. They were now keenly aware that their parents with worried looks, would often try to secretly listen to the news on their TV or radio during the day. Then they would talk about it away from the children's ears, always in hushed voices. Their faces now often looked concerned and anxious, especially when they listened to the President's daily TV address to the nation.

Mum, Lena, kept working from home as a dressmaker, but was taking on lots of extra orders to try and save some extra money – just in case….

Dad, Ivan, still left daily for his work as an engineer at the local steel plant. However, he knew that his days there were probably numbered. Soon it was most likely he would be called upon to join up with the local Ukrainian army volunteers. Their job was to be on guard and defend their town from Russian attacks and any further advances of the Russian army.

The children were still both attending school on the day Sveta's windows were broken. The teachers deliberately tried to not mention the war with Russia, so the kids would not become too worried.

However, now it seemed that the war had arrived in Sveta's family's back yard. Like other schools in the war zones, their local school would probably start daily bomb or air raid drills for the children, just in case…..

Then everyone would know what to do immediately, if a missile ever directly hit the school….

After the bombing of the neighbours' building, the response was similar to what had happened already in many parts of Ukraine. School attendances suddenly dropped in their area. Some parents no longer permitted their children to walk to school. Many were just kept at home to study on alone.

Some men quickly despatched their wives and children to the railway station, so they could leave on the next train to travel to some foreign border and a peaceful, safer nation…..

For how long, nobody knew. The government had forbidden the younger men to leave the country, so they all had to stay on and fight where necessary. But thousands of women and children were streaming out.

Up to that dreadful morning, Sveta's parents had not made any definite evacuation plans. They were just hoping that the conflict would soon blow over and that the advancing Russian troops would withdraw. This happened with the first major army advance to surround and conquer Kiev, the nation's capital. It had been a fizzer and finally the Russian troops all pulled out. But now that appeared less likely in their home region, as the Russians had steadily moved forward and already taken over many towns just like theirs. Sudden changes were around the corner and Sveta wasn't quite sure what was going to happen next.

CHAPTER 2

F ortunately, as the light of the day increased, the sound of explosions ceased. To distract a little from the seriousness of the situation, Lena said "Sveta please take Patch outside to the toilet." Poor Patch their dog, was cowering under the bed.

In cities or towns in Ukraine, everybody lives in a flat in a large, grey cement apartment block. Ukrainians love pets. Their dogs have to learn very early that they only get taken outside, to do their 'business' once in the morning and once at night. This usually involves a trip down many floors in the elevator, where often many dog owners and their animals are suddenly face to face in a very small, confined space.

This can get challenging! Cats get a better deal, as they usually have an indoor litter box.

So, Sveta took the still trembling Patch downstairs in the lift that morning. Fortunately, nobody else was around then and

Patch soon settled down to his usual routine. After he had done his 'business', he enjoyed some free time off the leash, exploring and sniffing around their yard and beyond, as it was not winter. In winter snow is everywhere. In that season, he usually wanted to just get back inside as quickly as possible and didn't explore much.

However, this day he disappeared from Sveta's sight for over 5 minutes. She wasn't too worried as this was quite normal for him. He always returned, as breakfast usually followed his short toilet break outside. She called out repeatedly, "Patch, Patch, where are you? Come back to me!"

Soon Patch emerged from behind a bush, somewhere near where the neighbours' block of flats had been bombed. His tail was wagging madly. He seemed to be carrying something coloured in his mouth. He dropped it excitedly at Sveta's feet. To her absolute horror, she realized it was a small torn child's T shirt, soaked in blood.

Screaming loudly, "No! No! No!" she scooped up Patch in her arms and ran back into the safety of the building. By the time they got out of the lift and entered the front door of their flat, she was still screaming loudly, because what she had seen was so horrible....

"It was soooo gross and disgusting!" she yelled. "Patch had a kid's T shirt dripping with red blood in his mouth!"

Her parents' faces were suddenly filled with a strange mixture of sadness and horror too. Nobody even wanted to consider who the T shirt might have belonged to......

Ivan Sveta's father, then began to really freak out. His anger against the Russian troops erupted, quickly overwhelming his mind and thoughts. He exploded with rage. "Those blasted Russians need to go to hell!"

But inside, he was also suddenly feeling a kind of urgent protectiveness towards his wife and children. Unexpectedly, he then declared, "The time has come for you to flee all this danger and violence here."

"Tomorrow you must all go on a train to somewhere in the West, where fighting is less intense."

Sveta suddenly realised this incident with Patch had opened a door she didn't want to go through. She certainly didn't want to leave the only home she'd ever known. She loved her school, her teachers and her sweet friends.

No, she would not be sent away that easily. She tried unsuccessfully to quickly sow some doubt into her story. Half crying, she insisted, "Dad, perhaps I didn't see it properly. Perhaps the little kid just had a really big nosebleed… Perhaps someone had just used the kid's old T shirt as a rag for red paint."

However, she knew in her heart, this was most unlikely, as there had been clearly so much fresh blood on it that attracted Patch.

Wailing, she quickly tried another approach, "Dad, we can't leave you here all alone. We all want to stay together as a family and help defend our village and land!"

But it was to no avail. Ivan had decided and none of his daughter's wails or his son's sobs could change his mind that day.

Lena, Sveta's Mum, decided to distract the family from their sudden conflict and rising fears. She tried to declare cheerfully "I still have a big pot of borsch on the stove, leftover from last night. Let's all go to the kitchen and have some now for breakfast!" Nobody seemed that keen but they followed her into the kitchen.

Borsch is the name of a typical Ukrainian meal enjoyed for breakfast, lunch or dinner. It's a red, thick, yummy beetroot and cabbage soup, with usually lots of other vegetables and sometimes meat. It gets cooked for quite some time to develop its deep flavour. Then it is usually served with a big dollop of 'smetana' (sour cream), on top.

So, all the family sat down to a hearty bowl of borsch with some crusty bread. Nobody said much. The borsch was still good, but not able to completely soothe and melt away all the confusion and uncertainty they now felt in their hearts. Sveta was hoping her school friends might give her some advice on how to turn around her dad's decision.

CHAPTER 3

That day at school, Sveta remained in a very bad mood. Her friends seemed to be in the same boat of uncertainty, with their dads also starting to talk about the possibility of them leaving. That night, she tried and tried to convince her father, that it would be better for them all to stay together in their village.

"Come on Dad, please give us another week or so at least. My teacher says those Russians are going to withdraw soon!" This was a bit of an exaggeration or almost a white lie, but Sveta felt it might help her side of the argument. But Ivan was unmoved and stuck to his original decision.

"You definitely have to leave the next day for safety reasons alone," he explained.

"Sveta, we can no longer trust the Russians in anything they say. They promised to not target civil sites, but their words are clearly were meaningless lies!" Sveta hung her head and whimpered.

"Go to your room Sveta now, and start packing your most important things in your backpack, together with lots of clean underwear and warm clothing."

"But Dad, when can we come back? Please tell me!" she implored him with tears in her eyes.

She couldn't believe the stony silence she kept receiving back, when she then asked repeatedly, where exactly they would be going and for how long. The truth was, nobody really knew the answers to these questions....

When her mother eventually checked her backpack, Lena couldn't believe it. "Sveta, you must be more practical and pack only useful and necessary things!" she said gently.

Mum removed the 4 bottles of Sveta's favourite coloured nail polishes, her slime making kit and all her toy pony collection, which admittedly was quite bulky. They were replaced with lots of her school books and more clothes. As tensions were already running high, Sveta just bit her lip and sobbed silently.

She begged her mother to at least include her favourite rag doll, Yulia that she had always kept close since childhood. Lena was also super busy that day, packing her own backpack, a little backpack for Sergy and a medium sized suitcase that they would all share. She made sure she included a big bag of bread for 'snacks.'

In Ukraine, bread is very important. It is their symbol for life and hope. No important event ever happens without bread. People are often first welcomed officially with salt and bread when they arrive at a new place. Ukrainians say they never feel full after eating a meal, unless it includes a good lot of bread. So Lena took lots of bread for their trip, just in case…..

Sveta knew from experience that trains from their town left early each morning for the capital Kiev. It was a journey of a couple of hours. Basically, you had to go to Kiev first, before catching any long-distance trains to get anywhere else. So, the next morning, the little family found themselves at the local railway station platform at 8 o'clock sharp.

Fortunately, it was still summer, so it was not very cold yet, although the sky was grey and miserable. Papa Ivan looked very sad and grim. Sveta also noticed her mother repeatedly wiping tears from the corner of her eyes, but also trying to smile and look happy, as though they were going on some sort of holiday. Sveta knew it was not the time to ask more questions, so she just kept quiet.

Sergy didn't understand everything, but he knew that it wasn't the moment to cry any more or have a tantrum. He clutched Patch tightly, who was going with them. Sadly, Ginger was staying back in the flat with Ivan. Finally, Sergy kept asked pitifully, "But when can we come home?" However, nobody was answering him....

They all managed to find their seats inside the carriage and sat down in silence. It was obvious that the train was far more packed than normal and everyone seemed rather stressed. Ivan on the platform, quickly found the window where they were sitting. Before the train pulled away from the platform, he reached out and put his big palm on the window pane next to them. Lena responded immediately by placing her palm on his, although now the thick glass window was between them.

No more words could be exchanged, but there was really nothing more to say. Sveta thought she also saw tears running down her father's cheeks, before the train sped off and he was out of sight. Sergy, for what seemed like the tenth time, asked again in a little sad voice, "When are we coming back home again?" Once again there was no response.

Finally seated, Sergy snuggled into Lena, who pretended to doze off. Sveta was left all alone, just with her own thoughts. At this stage, she felt a strange mixture of confusion. But soon inside, a strong anger suddenly swamped her emotions. She was angry that nobody would answer any of their questions. She was angry because she didn't have time to go and see her special school friends or teachers before leaving. She was especially very angry at the Russians and Putin, for causing all this suffering and the terrible war she was now living through in her young life.

She looked at the other passengers. Many people had no seat. They were swaying wildly, as they stood sombrely in the aisle of the carriage. Few spoke. Most people had blank faces or just like her Mum, were wiping away the odd silent tear that managed to escape.

As the train finally pulled into the outer suburbs of the city of Kiev, she saw familiar blue and yellow flags flying everywhere. Ukraine's flag, with a wide stripe of yellow and blue on top, simply represents the thousands of golden wheat fields in their nation, lying underneath the blue skies of heaven.

However, Sveta then started noticing strange things she'd never seen before on her previous trips to the capital. Abandoned Russian tanks, blackened car bodies and lots of assorted rusting metal rubbish, now littered the edge of many parts of the highways leading to the main railway station. It was not a pretty sight, but clear evidence of a war, far too close for comfort. Time to reach into Mum's plastic bag for a comforting piece of bread. She usually was excited visiting Kiev, and began to feel a mixture of that same excitement jostling and trying to push out all her fears and anger. What fortunes would the big smoke of Kiev bring to Lena, the kids and Patch?

CHAPTER 4

As they pulled into Kiev railway station, it was obvious things were far from normal. It was overflowing with thousands of anxious people, mostly just women and children. They all had long, worried faces. Numerous animals, both cats and dogs, pulled on their short leashes, and were adding to the chaos, commotion and unusual smell.

Sveta asked Lena "What is going to happen to Ginger when Daddy's out fighting?"

Lena didn't answer the question once again, but sternly instructed Sveta to wait in a tiny cleared area with Sergy, Patch and all their luggage. She went to line up in the very long queue to buy train tickets to leave the country. They waited for over 2 hours, before an exhausted Lena returned with a refreshment for them all as well as the prized tickets.

Lena then sat everybody down and tried to explain glumly what was happening to the best of her ability.

"Look, we are going to get a train to Poland tomorrow evening. It will be a very long trip, about 9 hours to Lyviv, a city in western Ukraine near the border. That is providing there is no fighting or explosions across the tracks along the way. This could delay or stop our journey."

Sveta and Sergy just listened in silence. What else could they say, since she had obviously told them everything she knew.

Unfortunately, Lena couldn't get them in a sleeper carriage (with bed bunks), so they would just have to share a couple of upright seats together for the long journey. However, this also depended on whether they were lucky enough to grab them first, when everyone rushed to board the train.

In the western city of Lyviv, they would spend the next night somewhere.... "I'm not yet exactly sure where...." Her voice trailed off again....

The following day they would be travelling on to Poland on yet another train. Sveta of course, was full of questions again, wanting far more information than the basic facts that were given. However, she was quickly silenced by a very exhausted Lena, who abruptly indicated once again, that this was all she knew at that moment.

After waiting most of the day in Kiev, near the platforms packed with people, they finally managed to board their train for Lyviv train that evening. Sveta had pushed and shoved ahead of the most of the crowd, squeezing in through the tiniest of spaces, between sweaty passengers and hairy animals at the carriage door. Marvellously, she had been able to quickly secure two seats for them all.

She felt good about this and noticed that somehow, a lot of her previous boiling anger had shifted a bit and was slowly starting to melt away.

However, it seemed to be now replaced by a new big black cloud of intense fear. Dark fears seemed to be strangling her mind with many unanswered questions.

"Where will we end up?

Will we ever return to our town and our old friends?

Will dad die in the war?

Will I ever see him again?

Will Dad remember to feed Ginger?

What on earth will we all do in Poland, when we can't speak the language? "

The future seemed now to be like a big black hole, that swallowed every good thing she could think of.

An older Sveta might have recognised this new state of mind simply as deepening depression. Holding a stressed Patch even tighter, she sank down into her seat and began to cry. She knew full well that it would probably set Sergy off again, but she didn't care anymore.

Sergy now also smelt distinctly of poo. However, Sveta just didn't feel up to doing anything about it yet. When she looked over to her mother she noticed, to her horror, that she was accepting far too many glasses of the national alcoholic drink, vodka.

Someone in the carriage was generously sharing their glasses and a large vodka bottle around, as the train finally pulled away. Some passengers were celebrating their escape, but most were just drowning their sorrows. (Since the days of communism in Ukraine, when vodka could sometimes be used to pay workers, it is very widely used. A large bottle of vodka is still relatively cheap, -only around a dollar or two.)

Soon Lena, Sergy and even Patch dozed off with the rhythmic rocking of the train. Sveta by now, felt very alone, miserable and totally helpless. Suddenly, from the seat behind, came a cheery voice.

"Hello, I'm Catia, would you like a chocolate biscuit?"– it was her favourite kind. When she turned round to see more clearly, she saw a girl with shoulder length dark hair, about her age, but possibly a bit older. She was grinning at her.

Sveta immediately wondered if this girl was crazy. How could she possibly be smiling and seem so happy, in the midst of all the trauma and turmoil they were living. Catia quickly introduced herself further and came around to Sveta's seat.

She had noticed Sveta's tears and glum look, so asked "What's up?" Sveta thought it was such a stupid question, but slowly began to pour out her heart and worries to Catia, who listened very carefully.

CHAPTER 5

As Sveta spoke, a flood of tears ran down her cheeks like rivers. All the anxieties of the recent past, present and future poured out. The train sped on, with an almost comforting, continuous 'clickety clack', 'clickety clack' underneath. Its journey fortunately was uninterrupted by the war or any type of enemy attack that day. Thus, they had plenty of time to talk as it was such a long trip.

Sveta then asked Catia "Tell me a bit about your life and why you're leaving?"

To her amazement, Catia's story was far more dramatic and tragic than her own. Catia had lived in a village on the very outskirts of Kiev, where there had already been lots of close fighting, bombing and death around her.

Catia explained, "Our flat was totally destroyed by a direct missile, and most of our belongings were then burnt up by fire.

But worse than that, my father was badly wounded. He now has PTSD from the stress of all the violence he's experienced. He battles lots of nightmares and can no longer go to the front to fight. He is now only driving lorries of supplies to the battlegrounds, and picking up the wounded Ukrainian soldiers to bring them back to hospital."

She had Sveta's full attention, so she went on, "He prays always for the active soldiers as he goes.

My elder brother has also gone off to fight and defend our village. But one day, he received a direct hit in the chest from a Russian bullet that should have killed him. However, because he had his mobile phone in his top pocket, the bullet lodged in it and only gave him a slight skin wound."

Catia happily declared God had totally protected his life because of their family prayers.

Sveta didn't quite know what to make of all this talk about praying for the soldiers and God's protection. She didn't know how to pray for her own father, or even if there really was a God up there who listened. Her family wasn't very religious, just a bit traditional in those things. Twice a year, Christmas and Easter, her mother usually took her to the Russian Orthodox church service in town.

There, they went to burn a candle and kiss the feet of a statue that was some famous saint. She was not really sure what this all meant or what value it had, if any. When they occasionally listened to the priest giving a talk, nothing really made much sense. This was mainly because the message was always given in the ancient Russian language, which nobody now fully understood.

She listened respectfully to Catia, but then finally asked her outright, "Are you sure God really exists or is religion just a waste of time?"

Catia's big eyes shone as she answered enthusiastically, "Oh Sveta, God is soooo real and soooo powerful! He made the whole earth and one day will judge the whole world and everyone in it too."

"You can actually know God as your heavenly Father, when you receive His Son Jesus as your own personal Lord and Savior. Don't you know all about Jesus?"

Sveta wasn't really sure. She muttered "Wasn't Jesus the man who was once stuck on a cross?" But then she enquired sincerely, "What has all that to do with us now, in the middle of a war with Russia?"

Catia patiently explained, "God, the Father, sent His Son Jesus to come down from heaven to earth and die for our sins. It's because we humans are all sinners. That means when we die we can never go to heaven with God. We all need to ask Jesus in prayer, to forgive our sins and come and rule in our hearts and lives!"

Sveta interrupted, "But how can He really do this, if He is dead? – didn't He die on that cross Catia?"

"Yes, Sveta He did! But then, God the Father raised Him from the dead and He lives forevermore. When we become a Christian, His Spirit comes and really lives in us!"

She continued eagerly "He gives us His salvation and then answers our prayers! That also means He can strengthen us, help us, comfort us and guide us, as we walk forward in life with Him each day!"

"Don't you get it Sveta? Knowing Jesus as your Savior is so wonderful and important! Without Him we are all lost and helpless and can never get to heaven."

Sveta certainly felt very lost and helpless at that moment. She wanted to ask more questions, but Catia's mother was calling her. Catia got up to go to her mother, but took out of her purse a colourful card which she gave to Sveta. It had a picture of Jesus on it with his hands outstretched. It read '**I am the way, the truth and the life. Nobody comes to the Father, except by me**.' *John 14:6.* Wow she thought, "Those words are kind of powerful!" They seemed to almost jump out at her from the card as she read them over and over.

I AM THE WAY, THE TRUTH AND THE LIFE. NOBODY COMES TO THE FATHER, EXCEPT BY ME. JHON 14:6

CHAPTER 6

That day, the sun was setting quite late, around 9pm, as it was still summer in Ukraine. Sergy and Patch were already fitfully dozing with the rhythmic rocking of the train. Sveta listened in carefully when her mother finally managed to do some face time on her mobile with Ivan back at home.

"It's fine my love, I have kept safe, even though it's getting tougher daily. So good you all managed to get out, as it puts my mind at rest about your safety."

He clearly missed them all too, and went on to report that the missile attacks and fighting had intensified in their town.

As the sky became darker and darker, Sveta's mother fell asleep and then snored louder and louder, as all the conversations in the carriage slowly diminished.

Sveta held the little card from Catia tighter and tighter and read over the words again and again, until all the light faded.

She didn't fully understand what her new friend had been saying, but she knew she really needed some help and hope at this point.

Finally, she blurted out aloud "Jesus, if you are really real, like Catia says, forgive my sins, come into my life and help my family please! Amen." As an afterthought she quickly added, "Jesus, I think we need somewhere to stay in the city of Lyviv. It needs to be cheap as Mum is very worried about having enough money to live. Thanks Jesus!" After that, she drifted off.

She must have managed to sleep a few hours after that. She awoke just as the early dawn light was streaming in through the window. Somehow, she felt a bit different inside, even though nothing had really changed in their situation on the outside. Weirdly though, the black cloud of depression and hopelessness seemed to have lifted.

It was a very long train trip, and she reasoned it would be a good time to take Sergy with her to the toilet, before the massive queue began again. The carriages had been built for a maximum number of people. However, with the war they were carrying at least double that number. Sveta had already discovered early on that the toilets had turned into a disaster zone. The bowl opened directly onto the tracks below when you flushed. However, too many drunk people had missed the bowl totally on the swaying train. The mat at the base of the bowl was now swimming in urine and worse, and was very smelly.

"YUUUUK, how gross!" she muttered under her breath!" as she held her nose tightly and was extra careful where she stepped. But at least they had a toilet to go to! You just had to be very careful…..

When they returned to their seats, Sveta saw that Catia's mother was sitting in her seat talking to her mother Lena. She stood there quietly and respectfully, but also eager to catch some of their conversation.

Catia's mother Olga explained "I know a great place to stay in Lyviv overnight. It is in a church hall. They have lots of mattresses on the floor, and plenty of hot borsch and bread. Best of all, it is all free for Ukrainians fleeing the war."

Sveta couldn't believe her ears. Without doubt, Jesus had not only heard her prayer, but clearly answered it!

Olga went back to her seat so that Catia and Sergy could sit down again. They immediately saw their Mum looking a bit happier and less stressed. They all enjoyed an early breakfast of more dark bread rolls and the typical black tea with lemon and sugar from the thermos. It had surprisingly managed to retain quite a bit of its heat overnight.

Then Catia popped up beside them again, offering them all a chocolate biscuit to raise their spirits even higher.

In stumbling words, Sveta tried to explain to Catia how she had asked Jesus to come into her heart and life, very late the night before. The train was just pulling into the platform at Lyviv. There was no time to continue talking, but Catia's grin became even larger. It was still very early morning, and since western Ukraine was further away from most of the fighting in the war, things on the platform looked a lot less hectic compared to Kiev.

When they all finally managed to exit the station in Lyviv, with their heap of luggage and animals (Catia had a cat in a carrycase too), there was a taxi rank with taxis waiting. In Ukraine, taxis are relatively cheap as many people don't have cars.

This means though, that they are very competitive. Best of all, they don't have rules about how many people they can take. They will try and pile in all the people, luggage or animals they can fit. Once, Sveta had even seen a large calf crammed in a taxi with the driver.

However, that day they chose a taxi that was a large old, dilapidated vehicle. Miraculously, it was capable of squeezing them all in. Olga negotiated the fare and told them all that it was a really short trip. So, it didn't matter that they were all sitting on each other and a heap of backpacks, and with a complaining animal on the very top of each pile. What was going to happen in this new unknown big city? Would it change the path of their future forever?

CHAPTER 7

T he bedraggled, exhausted little group stepped out of the taxi and they were welcomed very warmly at the church hall door by a bunch of volunteers. Since the war had intensified, these people had clearly dedicated their daily lives to serving the thousands of Ukrainian refugees passing through their town to the Polish border.

This place was such a hub of activity, but a peaceful one, unlike the railway station chaos in Kiev. Volunteers were also constantly serving meals, answering phone calls and packing 10 or 11 trucks each day with supplies to go to the front. These went out daily with food supplies, blankets, bandages, and medicines to soldiers or needy people near the fighting zones who couldn't flee or leave.

Each day, thousands of refugees were streaming in to Lyviv city from the more eastern zones of the country, where fighting was far fiercer. Sveta found out later that most of the volunteers were strong Christians, like Catia and her Mum.

On arrival, they were all immediately presented with a hot, two-course meal. Then they were offered extra warm clothing, medicines or counsel, all for free. Finally, they were ushered into another big room that was set up with nearly 80 mattresses on the floor. There, they could safely leave their stuff and also sleep overnight. It was even better than Olga had briefly described earlier, and they were all very grateful to God for this wonderful provision.

"Thank-you Jesus!" Sveta whispered.

After the meal, someone asked about water for a shower or at least a wash. They then were led to the appropriate area. Catia and Sveta were able to obtain mattresses side by side, so they were soon deep in conversation again. Sveta wanted to hear more about how to pray 'properly' and what it really meant being a Christian.

Sveta also voiced some of her doubts to Catia. "Did Jesus really come into my heart when I prayed that prayer last night?" She asked quite earnestly.

"Were they just nice symbolic words that I spoke in my prayer? Because how could He have really entered my heart? He simply would be too big!"

Catia replied "No Sveta, it was the Spirit of Jesus, the Holy Spirit, who entered in your heart, not the physical Jesus.

She continued, "After His resurrection from the dead, He sat down in heaven at the right hand of God, the Father. And yes, He did really come into your heart when you invited Jesus to be your Savior!"

Sveta then asked if heaven was a real place. Catia nodded rather seriously. She was silent for about a minute and Sveta thought she could see tears starting to form in her big brown eyes.

When Sveta gently asked what was wrong, Catia responded. "Recently during the missile attack on our building, my 8-year-old cousin, Oleg was hit directly."

Sveta still didn't quite understand, so Catia sadly explained it in another way.

"Sveta, he was killed by the missile and has now gone to live permanently in heaven because he belonged to Jesus." Sveta was always full of questions and gently probed further, "But how do you know that heaven exists, if you can't see it or see Oleg anymore?"

Catia replied "In God's Word, the Bible, Jesus promised over and over, that when His true children die, they will enter heaven forever."

There was another large pause.

Then Catia added in a hushed voice, "The night after Oleg died, I couldn't stop crying. But that night I had a clear dream, in which I saw him alive in heaven, talking to Jesus and also another young boy from our village who died of leukemia last year. They are definitely in heaven now Sveta."

Later that day, the mothers, Lena and Olga, sat down on nearby mattresses too. They were sharing together their possible plans for the future. Olga with Catia and their cat in tow, were heading for a very small village, just across the border with Poland, because they had an old aunt living there. On the other hand, Lena knew nobody in Poland or any other country. She had already been thinking a lot about what would be best for her little family.

They were heading to the Polish border simply because it was the closest, safe nearby nation. Also, the cost of living was not too high in comparison to Ukraine. Sveta's mother's plan eventually became to get off their next train at the first BIG town in Poland. She reasoned that she had to be located in a place with a large population, so she could get enough dressmaking work to support them.

Sveta in particular, was devastated when she heard that Catia was destined to settle in a different place in Poland. She couldn't believe this could happen! She certainly didn't want to lose her new found friend.

She clung to Lena, screaming out to her mother "Please change your mind, please change your mind! I must be with Catia!"

But practical Lena would not budge and said to a tearful Sveta, "You've got to get over it darling, I need to work because we need to eat! It's that simple."

Sveta was so upset she went that night to the adults' prayer meeting in the church hall, to get God to change her mother's mind. She was sure God understood her reasoning and would bow to her very logical request. She couldn't imagine that God might have a different or better plan…..

CHAPTER 8

I n the morning, after a good night's sleep and a hearty breakfast of barley porridge, they all headed back to the Lyviv railway station. The mothers went to the ticket office to buy train tickets to cross the border and carry them into Poland and to their final destinations.

Everybody shared a taxi once again, and they were all getting on the same train at Platform 4. That looked like a good start! Sveta was sure God was going to intervene for her, so she wasn't as withdrawn as Catia. She apparently had sadly accepted that now, for practical and economic reasons, they would end up apart.

There were no problems with customs at the Polish border, even though nobody had passports or visas. The Polish government had declared that all Ukrainian refugees could have free, safe passage because of the war with Russia. The border was relatively close, just over an hour after starting off their journey.

Soon, Olga and Catia began to get their things ready to disembark.

With tears in her eyes, Catia handed Sveta her little children's Bible and said, "I promise to keep in touch with you dear friend, via messaging on Mum's mobile."

She added quickly, "Sveta, try to read a chapter every day of God's Word."

Sveta couldn't believe her ears. She was so upset, she started yelling and screaming "NOOOOO!"

She reached out to try and stop Catia's swift advance towards the door. But her mother had anticipated this, and roughly grabbed both her arms and forced her to sit back down on the seat.

Olga, Catia and the cat quickly stepped down onto the little platform, on the train's first stop at a tiny village. And the train then pulled away rather swiftly.

Sveta's mind was flooded again with both grief and anger. She wasn't sure who to be angry with.

Why didn't they choose to go with them to the bigger, better town?

Why hadn't her mother reconsidered their new location?

Why had God let her down by not answering her prayer?

Of course, Sveta was now in God's school of faith, kindergarten level. This first difficult lesson she had to learn was that God always answers our prayers.

But sometimes with a 'YES', sometimes with a 'NO', and sometimes with a 'WAIT' or 'I HAVE A BETTER WAY. However, God always has in mind the best plan for our lives, although He doesn't always tell us exactly what lies ahead.

Slowly Sveta slumped back into her seat, half whimpering and half sobbing in disbelief. Nobody was taking any notice of her. After a while, she started talking to God in a bit of an angry tone.

She first asked Him, "Why didn't You do something to make sure we all ended up together?"

She waited for an answer, at least a silent one, in her heart. But there was no response at all. All she could hear was the rhythmic 'clickety clack' of the train's forward movement. 'Clickety clack,' 'clickety clack' over and over.

However, after a while, she thought it sounded a bit different. Somehow, it seemed to sound more like 'trust in me,' 'trust in me' 'trust in me' over and over. Could it be that God was speaking back to her in this way? She wasn't sure at all at this stage, but she began to feel a kind of gentle peace in her heart.

It was quite the opposite of all the black despair she had felt just minutes before. Her mother was looking out the window and clearly didn't want to talk. So, she thought she might as well talk to God again and ask Him for something else, since He had provided so well for them all in Lyviv.

She bowed her head and quite reverently, prayed, "God, please provide a good, safe, cheap place for us to stay in our new town that we don't know yet."

Within another hour and a bit, it was their turn to get off the train, at a much larger station. Sveta had begun again to fight fearful dark thoughts. She remembered that in Poland, they speak Polish, not the Ukrainian language. How would she ever manage to communicate or go to school there?

As they lugged Blackie and all their luggage out of the train door, they were suddenly faced with a long line of mainly women, holding up big placards with things written on them. One lady was also offering everybody warm soup, as the temperature had dropped quite a bit. They all took the soup and started to read the placards.

Most of the placards were in Polish, and a few in English with a little Ukrainian or Russian language added. It seemed they were mostly Christian ladies, offering their homes and food for the refugees, free or for a small cost. Sveta scanned the placards, most of which didn't make much sense to her, and sent up a quick three-word prayer to God: "Jesus help us!"

Suddenly her eyes fell on a yellow placard written in Ukrainian. It was held up by a stout little woman right at the back. It read first of all 'welcome!' Then in smaller print was written 'Ukrainian family, you are welcome to come and live with me for as long as you like, or until the Lord leads you out. I speak Ukrainian and will help you. Pets are welcome too!'

Sveta tugged her mother's sleeve madly and waved to the little stout grandmother, who pushed forward in the crowd to encircle the little family with warm embraces. A new chapter of their lives had begun and a new walk of faith for Sveta. Although, everything ahead was strange and uncertain still, she knew that Jesus her Saviour was with them. He was God, powerful, and wise, so He would work it all out somehow....

Deep in her heart Sveta knew that Jesus would now always be her 'way forward in life.' Somehow, she sensed He was enough for any adventures or misadventures that circumstances might throw in her path. After all, from now on, Jesus was HER way, HER truth, and HER life, just like Catia's little card had said.

COMPREHENSION STUDY BOOK

CHAPTER 1 – "SOMETIMES THINGS CHANGE OVERNIGHT."

1) What one event would change forever the life of Sveta and her family?

....

....

....

2) How did the different members of Sveta's family react to this incident?

....

....

....

3) How would you feel, if very early morning, the room shook and your window broke?

....

....

....

4) Would members of your household act the same way Sveta's family did, or differently?

....

....

....

5) What was Sveta's life in Ukraine like before the war with Russia?

....

....

....

CHAPTER 2 – "WHAT A HORRIFIC DISCOVERY!"

1) What gruesome discovery did Patch make outside that morning?

....

....

....

2) What did this suggest might have happened in the next-door block of flats?

....

....

....

3) Sveta felt this incident "had opened a door she did not want to go through." What exactly was this door that she didn't want to enter?

....

....

....

4) What were some of Sveta's arguments to her dad for not leaving their town?

....

....

....

5) In what way did Lena, Sveta's Mum, try to reduce the tension between Sveta and her father?

....

....

....

6) When you see people's emotions rapidly rising in a conflict, what is one way you can think of to help them to calm down a bit?

....

....

....

CHAPTER 3 – "A VERY UNCERTAIN ROAD AHEAD."

1) What things did Sveta first pack, that her mother considered were not practical?

....

....

....

2) Why did Ivan, Sveta's father insist on sending his family away?

....

....

....

3) Why couldn't Sveta's parents tell the children exactly where they were going?

....

....

....

4) Explain in your own words why bread is so important to Ukrainians.

....

....

....

5) At this point in the story, why did Sveta feel so angry?

....

....

....

6) If you had to suddenly leave your home the next day, what 5 important things would you make sure were included in your back pack? Why?

....

....

....

CHAPTER 4 – "WILD, FLUCTUATING FEELINGS."

1) How did the Kiev railway station look very different to normal, on the day they arrived?

....

....

....

2) What plan forward did Sveta's Mum explain that they would follow?

....

....

....

3) What happened soon to Sveta's feelings of anger?

....

....

....

4) Why did Sveta think that Catia was crazy or stupid at first?

....

....

....

5) How did Catia manage to help lift Sveta's dark mood and feelings?

....

....

....

6) When you are feeling very sad or depressed, what things help you to feel a little better?

....

....

....

CHAPTER 5 – "DELVING DEEP FOR ANSWERS!"

1) Had Catia suffered similar things to Sveta? Was her suffering greater or less?

....

....

....

2) What exactly happened to Catia's father and what is PTSD?

....

....

....

3) Why didn't Catia's brother die?

....

....

....

4) What did Catia explain to Sveta about God and Jesus?

....

....

....

5) What did Catia's little card say about Jesus?

....

....

....

6) Do you think that you have a personal relationship with Jesus, as your personal Saviour and friend, or do you feel more like Sveta felt at this point?

....

....

....

CHAPTER 6 – "WOW! GOD IS REAL AND ACTUALLY ANSWERS US."

1) What exactly did Sveta pray to Jesus before falling asleep?

....

....

....

2) Why was going to the toilet on a Ukrainian train, so challenging for Sveta?

....

....

....

3) How was the second part of Sveta's prayer answered the next morning?

....

....

....

4) What did Sveta quickly tell Catia she had done the night before? What was Catia's reaction?

....

....

....

5) How do most people in Ukraine travel to and from a railway station? Why is it so convenient?

....

....

....

6) Have you ever shared with others about God and Jesus? Why is this important?

....

....

....

CHAPTER 7 – "REAL CHRISTIANS ARE INCREDIBLE."

1) What was going on in the church hall in Lyviv where they all stayed the night?

....

....

....

2) Each day what exactly did the trucks do, that travelled to the front where there was fighting?

....

....

....

3) Did the physical Jesus come into Sveta's heart when she prayed? How exactly?

....

....

....

4) What reasons did Catia give for heaven being a real place?

....

....

....

5) How were Lena and Olga's plans for the future different?

....

....

....

6) Why did Sveta go to the adults' prayer meeting in the church that night?

....

....

....

CHAPTER 8 – "YES, NO, WAIT OR I HAVE A BETTER PLAN."

1) When they all left Lyviv, why was Sveta not as sad as Catia?

....

....

....

2) What was Catia's final present to Sveta and why was it so important?

....

....

....

3) Does God always answer all our prayers with a 'Yes' and just always give us what we want?

....

....

....

4) When Sveta was angry after Catia got off the train, how did God speak to her?

....

....

....

5) What were some of Sveta's fears about the future?

....

....

....

6) How did God answer Sveta's prayer about finding a place to live in Poland?

....

....

....

7) What should you do at moments when things in your future seem so uncertain and filled with unanswered questions?

....

....

....

EASY WORD SEARCH!

Find the words below in the puzzle. Circle each one you find.
How long does it take you to find them all?
The words can go in any direction, - vertical horizontal or diagonal.
The words can also share letters as they cross over each other.

```
H E A V E N D Q S A R E T S
A A V F F I N A L S N D S V
B L N I F D F W S I X O U E
H O O R G E A N T V K G R T
I N M N U R I U D L O C T A
G E L B E S O L I V I C S S
H R N L I R S F E V A T O D
Z C I O A N S I E B N R R I
F H H E I S G H A E U B R A
H T I A F S I R R N I D O R
R I O P O C S E C E V A W Y
S A F U L S V E G A G G U L
O F T E T E Y K R R T U V T
U H Y A R S N I W P A I P A
P S A L V A T I O N E I A N
Z N I G H T M A R E J D L K
```

all	alone	alone
belief	bombing	Catia
chaos	civil	cold
depression	faith	faith
final	forgive	God
grief	heaven	high
luggage	nightmare	raids
rail	reverent	routine
run	Russian	sad
safe	salvation	sorrow
soup	south	Sveta
tank	trust	vehicle
visa	war	wave
wins		

MORE DIFFICULT WORD SEARCH!

Find the words below in the puzzle. Circle each one you find.
How long does it take you to find them all?
The words can go in any direction, - vertical horizontal or diagonal.
The words can also share letters as they cross over each other.

```
X  D  C  Z  I  D  R  G  N  Y  I  N  M  F  B  U  D  G  E  W  P  S  M  U
Y  Z  A  R  C  A  A  I  N  G  F  E  R  R  S  N  O  I  S  O  L  P  X  E
Y  I  U  U  E  C  R  M  K  A  U  I  O  I  A  V  W  C  L  U  A  N  Y  N
K  K  F  F  G  G  E  B  A  D  B  G  F  G  B  Y  H  U  F  N  T  C  T  L
U  K  R  A  I  N  I  A  N  G  E  H  N  H  E  R  A  F  M  D  F  I  I  U
E  L  B  A  R  E  S  I  M  S  E  B  I  T  I  K  R  S  A  E  O  T  L  F
T  T  W  C  Y  P  N  M  H  L  T  O  R  S  S  E  H  U  T  D  R  C  A  E
M  A  U  Z  A  Z  O  I  C  D  I  R  T  I  E  U  E  Y  T  R  M  E  T  C
S  O  N  C  C  O  F  A  C  T  Z  I  A  T  S  C  P  P  R  Z  E  H  I  A
G  T  E  T  D  T  R  S  H  I  A  C  N  N  I  I  O  E  E  J  A  S  P  E
S  U  R  Y  R  I  R  U  E  N  D  U  S  F  G  V  U  E  S  G  J  S  S  P
E  V  N  A  M  U  E  O  A  S  L  E  F  I  D  E  T  L  S  O  E  W  O  V
R  A  H  B  N  E  M  I  P  O  Q  O  M  M  L  S  R  S  U  Y  F  I  H  V
I  Y  P  T  G  G  L  X  V  R  J  A  U  H  S  E  S  R  A  F  F  F  H  L
O  S  T  U  I  I  E  N  S  Y  M  B  O  L  I  C  N  O  B  P  B  T  J  Q
U  A  F  H  G  A  J  A  P  E  R  P  T  S  S  E  K  C  R  E  D  I  U  G
S  E  N  H  G  Q  F  J  U  L  E  E  A  Y  Y  N  S  W  E  G  B  L  N  E
R  M  T  G  M  I  S  S  I  L  E  F  X  C  A  R  R  I  A  G  E  R  Q  E
E  G  A  R  E  T  M  Y  Q  J  E  H  I  T  P  R  A  C  T  I  C  A  L  L
R  V  H  C  S  R  O  B  V  I  L  L  A  G  E  W  P  T  A  E  P  E  R  F
```

Anger	anxious	bang
borsch	budge	carriage
cheap	Christian	crazy
damage	debris	explosion
faith	fare	fear
flee	fright	grin
gross	guide	gun
hectic	help	hope
hospitality	inform	journey
light	mattress	medicine
mighty	miracle	miserable
missile	moody	neighbor
office	past	peaceful
platform	practical	pray
rage	refugee	repeat
safe	serious	shift
silence	sleepy	space
strange	stranger	stress
swift	symbolic	tank
tantrum	taxi	Ukrainian
village	volunteer	wounded

WRITING YOUR OWN NARRATIVE

Choose one of the following 3 questions to write a 500-word essay on below-

1. Write a narrative in the first person of your own real-life experience of moving house in your own city or moving inter-state in your own country.

2. Use your imagination to write an essay from the viewpoint of 5-year-old Sergy, leaving Ukraine on the train to flee the Russians.

3. Pick a country of your choice where you perhaps would like to move to in the future. Research in Google about the climate, customs, religion and food. Describe these briefly and how these would affect you living in this new country.

ART AND DESIGN

Choose one of the 3 art options below to create your own poster.

1. Draw a picture of Sveta sitting in her new room in Poland, with Patch the dog.
Also show what she can see out her new, big window.

2. Draw or create a collage from pictures of items, that you would pack in your suitcase to take with you, when you are relocating. (Include 10-15 items.)

3. Imagine you are leaving your homeland. Draw both, the outline of the country you are leaving and moving to. Include a picture of the flag and traditional food dish of both countries on your poster.

HELP CHANGE THE WORLD BY PRAYING THAT:

1) The many thousands of Ukrainians fleeing the homes will hear the gospel and receive Jesus as their Saviour.

2) The many young men and women going out to fight the war, (both Ukrainians and Russians), will also hear the gospel and receive Jesus as their Saviour.

3) The war in Ukraine will soon be over.

4) Many countries will continue to help with funds so the nation can rebuild.

TO CONTACT THE AUTHOR/ILLUSTRATOR

Please contact Julia Love via email at
julialove10@yahoo.com and
Angelica Rodriguez via email at
anglikbarbery@gmail.com